Introvert Power.

Achieve Happiness in Life by Applying Simple Success Principles for Introverts

Katherine Curtis

0

Table of Contents

www.ingramcontent.com/pod-product-compliance
Lightning Source LLC
Chambersburg PA
CBHW070936220526
45468CB00005B/1800

* 9 7 8 1 7 9 7 4 6 6 7 6 7 *

Chapter 1

Are you an Introvert?

Over the years, introverts have been tagged loners, reclusive, shy and deemed unsuitable for leadership positions because of their perceived lack of charisma. But adult introverts are not the only ones who suffer from negative perception. Even today, introversion is being discouraged in children. A prime example of this is a scenario that many parents of introverts face regularly – their child's teacher has expressed concern because the child in question is not as outgoing as others or keeps to themselves. These complaints by well-meaning people in the child's life further drive home the message that there is something wrong, and unnatural about being an introvert.

Being perceived as quiet, delicate and odd shouldn't define introverts as weak, boring and extremely fragile people. There are a

Chapter 6

Introvert Issues: Own and Tackle your problems

great many stellar qualities lurking deep within that calm exterior. There is a fun side to being an introvert too! Dig through the pages of this book and you'll discover this fun side, unlearning some traditional ideas about introverts along the way. If you're introverted, you're sure to uncover and enjoy incredible truths about your personality.

Are you an introvert?

To be candid, very few introverts have ever been asked that question. Instead, they are asked questions like:

'Why are you so quiet?'

'Don't you get bored and lonely?'

'Are you angry?'

'Do you ever have fun?'

'Do you have any friends?'

While these questions are tiring for introverts, it often comes out of a poor understanding of introversion. Therefore, the next section of this workbook is important. It will address what introversion is not.

What Introversion Is Not

Introversion is not depression

Unfortunately, introversion is often wrongly associated with depression. Because many introverts tend to keep to themselves and are energized by spending time alone, they are often labeled as depressed. When family members or friends tag introverts as depressed, this can be further isolating for introverts who generally already feel isolated. Yes, introverts can feel isolated, and this often stems from not being understood by the people who matter the most to them. While introverts can also suffer from depression, introversion and depression are entirely different.

Introversion is not being antisocial or asocial

Another common misconception when it comes to introversion is equating it with being antisocial. While it is possible for an introvert to be antisocial, the two states of mind are quite different. A major difference between an introvert and an antisocial individual is that an antisocial person behaves in a manner that is against social norms and which is also often harmful to those around them. In contrast, introverts are people who simply love their own company and get energized by spending time alone. Asocial individuals, on the other hand, dislike socializing and try to avoid it. Honestly, sometimes the lines between all these personalities blur so how do you know if you're an introvert?

Let's use a simple analogy to help you know for sure.

There are lots of things you can do with your phone. You can play games, chat with your friends, video call your grandparents, read an article, and work on the go. But first, you have to charge it fully, right?

For introverts, that charging happens when they're alone. They recharge their life batteries by spending time on their own. When their 'batteries' are full, they can engage in quite a number of activities. Even some activities which seem extroverted in nature. The difference, however, is that while an extrovert would be energized by spending time in highly stimulating environments like a large party, the introvert's 'battery' would be running down during that same party, and sooner rather than later. If you are always excited to go to events and then get tired before they're even halfway through, you just might be an introvert.

Introversion is not synonymous with being rude

While every introvert has a unique personality, one behavioural trait common in this group is their inability to tolerate small talk. They are not deliberately being rude but tend not to have the ability to sustain conversation that doesn't seem important. This and other factors may be construed as rudeness. It does not mean that an introvert cannot be rude, but rudeness shouldn't be considered synonymous with being an introvert.

What is an introvert?

Now that we know what introversion is not, let us briefly look at what introversion is.

- Introversion is the compelling need to enjoy one's own company and solitude. Introverts are more likely to engage themselves in activities that encourage introspection.

- Introverts enjoy activities like writing, reading, pet sitting, painting, watching videos online for hours, visiting libraries, museums or art theaters and meditating. These activities require minimum stimulation and interaction with other people.

- Introverts are often thoughtful people. They are much likely to thoroughly think things through before speaking.

- When it comes to friends, introverts prefer quality over quantity. They prefer small groups of friends to large groups.

- Being around lots of people drains the energy of introverts.

- Introverts are usually quiet. This is often related to the 'energy' issue. When introverts deem a conversation as not deep or meaningful, they tend to remain quiet and avoid it.

- Introverts learn by observation. Unlike extroverts who are more likely to learn by trial and error, introverts learn best by watching.

- Introverts prefer jobs that allow for independence. Jobs that require lots of social interaction and team effort are usually not of interest to introverts as they prefer working alone.

Chapter 2

What are your strengths as an introvert?

Ask most introverts and they'll tell you about a time when they were made to feel abnormal because of their innate need for solitude. This chapter discusses the strengths of introverts, and since introverts are thought to be quiet and shy, we should kick off with a strength that might seem quite bewildering at first.

Great conversationalists!

As odd as that may sound, Introverts are in fact, great conversationalists. Not just in the sense of staying in tune with the point of discussion, they are also good listeners and what is a conversation without listening? Their outward demeanour may not seem like it, but more often than not introverts display a readiness to listen, pay apt attention and think deeply before speaking. Obviously, introverts do not eagerly initiate conversations with those who they aren't very familiar with. However, they are very good at having and sustaining great conversations with people they connect with, like intimate friends, families and mentors. As an introvert, your distaste for small talks and public attention shouldn't put you at the rear of the crowd. Your craving for deep and meaningful conversations is valid but you never know where you might find that, so it's okay to give people a chance. It is okay to take part in small talk from time to time. Sometimes, this type of conversation can pave the way to more meaningful discussions.

Observation

Introverts are especially blessed with the ability to stay focused a lot more than people with other personalities. Why? Because introverts learn by observation. The good news is that when these traits are channeled to the business and educational field, success is never far off! As an introvert, think back to the times when you noticed things that others didn't immediately see. Your ability to focus and observe more critically is definitely a blessing, and when directed toward your career, a relationship, or even education, it can be extremely beneficial.

Creativity

Solitude is the incubator of creative ideas and nobody loves solitude like the introvert. Writing seems to be an ingrained speciality in introverts. Many introverts have second thoughts about expressing their thoughts verbally and therefore turn to writing for self-expression. Writing, however, is not the only place where introverts thrive. There are successful introverts in every field from computer programming to acting.

Prioritizing

This is one trait and strength of the introvert personality that makes them very good employees. Because of this trait, an introverted person is able to have a work and life balance. Introverts are self-motivated and can get the job done without being micromanaged. In fact, they don't like to be micromanaged.

Team Players

Surprising isn't it? Introverts crave autonomy, especially in carrying out their jobs, yet they can still be team players. For a team to work there must be unity and collaboration. While everyone is struggling to be seen and heard, the introvert isn't. Peace and unity are more important to them than being heard. This doesn't mean they have nothing to contribute to the group. Introverts are more often than not filled with ideas.

Unique Leadership Skills

While introverts are not usually deemed leadership material, they do in fact, make great leaders. Leadership is much more than a resounding voice, charming smile and a firm handshake. Introverts have the innate ability to foster deep, meaningful relationships; they are attuned to emotional cues and are able to pick up cues that might not be voiced. This is essential when there is a common goal to be achieved. Also, because they do not seek out the spotlight, they give their teammates the opportunity to shine and feel valued.

Over thinking

This might seem like a disadvantage, and sometimes it can be. But, the fact that introverts go through things countless times in their mind can also be advantageous. Why? Because, by over thinking, introverts can uncover potential problems. This can be very valuable in a work setting. As long as the introvert does not let over thinking prevent them from acting, over thinking can be a strength.

Good Listeners

This can come in handy for introverts at work, school or even in a leadership position. Listening is an important part of communication. If this trait is harnessed properly, the introvert can excel in almost every area of life.

Chapter 3

Understanding the Psyche of an Introvert vs. Extrovert

The discovery of various personalities has triggered some debate on which personality is superior. The answer is neither. Each one of these personalities has its own strengths and weaknesses. Introverts and extroverts should learn to appreciate and respect the differences in each other.

There are many distinctions between introverts and extroverts. These differences mostly stem from the sensitivity of each of these personalities to dopamine and acetylcholine, two powerful neurotransmitters that can affect us both physically and psychologically. Everything from appetite to mood is affected by these neurotransmitters.

Dopamine is a feel-good neurotransmitter, it rewards us with feelings of happiness when we take part in certain activities. Because of this pleasurable feeling, we are spurred to repeat those activities that brought us the feeling of pleasure. Some studies have shown that extroverts have a lesser sensitivity to dopamine, meaning they need more of it to feel happy. Introverts, on the other hand, are more sensitive to dopamine and easily get overwhelmed by activities (such as extreme sports) that lead to an increase in dopamine.

Acetylcholine is also linked to pleasure, but the type of pleasurable feeling it gives is more subtle than that gotten from dopamine. Acetylcholine makes us feel relaxed and focused. It enables us to be reflective, and think. Because extroverts have more dopamine receptors (which in turn make them need higher levels of dopamine to feel good), the pleasure brought about by acetylcholine release is not as intense or desirable to them. They need more external stimulation to feel invigorated and thrive.

Extroverts feel more at home when they're surrounded by many interesting people. It's a lot like sapping energy from a crowd to power up effectively. It is a different story for introverts, however. Not surprisingly, when introverts get too much stimulation from the outside world, they tend to become very stressed and tired. In a way, it's like passing large electrical currents to a very tiny circuit board. The circuit board will eventually burn out in no time. That being said, there are times when introverts and extroverts will need to move out of their comfort zones and try to keep up in different conditions that might seem unsuited to their personality type.

The right mental attitude: Introverts and extroverts

Basically, everyone has an attitude. To a very large extent, attitude defines everything. It influences the way we think, and primarily the way we respond to different situations.

The power of a positive mental attitude is remarkably unlimited. As an extrovert or introvert, you can effectively develop the right mental attitude towards all things: family, work, relationships and society. It all depends on how willing you are to work at it.

Types of Introverts

Introverts have been recently subdivided into four groups. Knowing what type of introvert you are can be instrumental in getting the most out of your life. The four groups are:

The Social Introvert:

This type of introvert doesn't shy away from social events (it should be noted here that shyness and introversion are synonymous). They might enjoy spending time out with friends and acquaintances more than other types of introverts. They usually prefer small groups of people to large groups. They are adept at building meaningful relationships.

The Thinking Introvert:

This type of introvert spends a lot of time in their head. They don't mind being in a crowd, but they'll spend a huge portion of that time lost in their own thoughts. These types are very creative and have a vivid imagination. Thinking introverts can spend too much time in their minds to the detriment of social interactions. Therefore, they should endeavour to set out a specific time for thinking and journaling so that when they're in the company of others, they can enjoy other people's company, knowing they have a set time for thinking alone.

The Anxious Introvert:

These are the type of introverts that feel awkward in social gatherings or in a crowd. They tend to go back home after a social gathering and over analyze all the things they think they said or did wrong. They worry about how they're perceived by others and this is a major cause of their introversion. Despite the obvious limitation of the over analyzing introvert, a few strengths of theirs include attention to detail, self-sufficiency and the ability to plan ahead.

The Restrained Introvert:

These introverts think before they act or speak. While the thinking introvert is more creative in thinking, this introvert is more analytical. A unique strength of theirs is seeing the bigger picture. They take some time to make decisions, and notice details people would not normally notice. In order to thrive, these introverts need a while to make decisions.

Chapter 4

Communicating better as an introvert

Our coexistence with other humans is mainly possible because we communicate. We communicate to pass on and receive information. But it goes way deeper than that. We communicate to feel loved and show love, we also communicate because we feel inclined to, that is only natural. The urge for humans to want to communicate is innate. In this chapter, there will be no theoretical analysis of what communication is or isn't. The focus here will be on how introverts can communicate better.

Anyone can learn to communicate better, including introverts. Yes, introverts do abhor small talk and would rather keep to themselves, but just like every other personality, introverts crave connections and good conversation. Below are some practical suggestions on how an introvert can communicate better and even initiate conversations.

Learn to communicate correctly

Pick the Right Time

Timing is very important when it comes to initiating a conversation. Imagine you've just been kicked out of your car by robbers and as you stare in bewilderment at the thieves speeding off in your car, a salesperson approaches, trying to sell you something. Would you be receptive to what the person has to say? Doubtful!

It's the same thing with conversations. You can't just dive into a conversation about the inner workings of your mind with someone who simply wants to make small talk. You have to be on the lookout for cues showing that the person is open to communication. Luckily for introverts, they're blessed with an eye that picks up cues that others wouldn't see right away.

Pick the Right Place

Communication for introverts also heavily relies on the environment. Picking a less stimulating environment is the best choice if you want to avoid draining your 'introvert battery.' For example, if you want to communicate in the workplace, it is best to avoid noisy places such as the lunch room.

Make An Effort

To truly master anything, you must make a consistent effort. Communication is no different. Listening already comes easily to introverts but what you can do to get more out of any conversation you listen to is ask questions. Instead of mulling over questions in your head, wait for a pause in the conversation and then chime in with your question. Because of the demeanour of introverts, it is easy for the person who is talking to feel like the introvert listening to them has zoned out or is not paying attention; by asking questions you prove that you were listening.

Face to Face

Many introverts prefer to text a person rather than call them. Text messages are great for casual conversations but when it comes to serious conversations, it is better to communicate face to face. This way, you can pick up nonverbal cues that you might not notice when you're having an electronic conversation. These cues can give you insights on whether or not your message is being communicated. While communicating, maintain eye contact, listen to what the other person says, and only interrupt if essential. While introverts tend to listen more, many people make the mistake of thinking that listening should be passive. You should listen with the aim of understanding the other person. If you don't understand, ensure you ask questions to clarify what is being said. You can also assist the listener to be an active listener by encouraging them to ask you questions if they need clarification.

Be Open to Learning

Learning communication is a continuous process. You'll come to find out that there's no one size fits all style for communication. For example, while some people prefer to have a conversation that slowly eases into the main issue, others prefer to grab the bull by the horns. Here are a few tips to help you communicate.

- Ask open-ended questions to get people to talk more.

- Avoid looking at your electronic device when someone else is talking.

- Be honest. If you feel you're not being heard, say so. If you feel the person is not paying attention, calmly let them know how you feel.

- Don't rush to fill in conversational pauses with more information. People sometimes need silence to process things.

- Don't jump to conclusions. Let people say what is on their mind before you draw a conclusion.

- Maintain an open posture. Avoid crossing your arms as it may send a message that you are not listening or that you disagree with what is being said. Also, avoid slouching.

- Maintain eye contact but look away from time to time. Steadily staring into someone's eyes can be very awkward.

Chapter 5

Practical Help

This chapter tackles real-life questions from introverts and provides answers.

- *"I feel like my introversion is keeping me from making the most of my life. Is there a way to change this nature and be more outgoing?"* ~George, 17.

Questions about how people can make the transition from introversion to extroversion is an exciting angle that many people want to explore. The question is, is that even possible? In previous chapters, it's been noted that being an introvert solely depends on how dominant your introversive traits are when compared with your extroversive traits. Scientifically, introversion can be genetically inherited. So, some introverts are just naturally predisposed to their traits. Nevertheless, those who were born as introverts may still display qualities of extroversion.

What if George was born an introvert? How would you propose he handles the situation?

It doesn't really matter if George was born as an introvert or if his environment and culture required him to become one. He is still just as introverted. The actual problem is what could have caused this desire to be more outgoing. Many things could have happened over time. A change in environment, new friends, a new taste of affection, peer pressure, new goals, family issues, religious views and teenage dreams could make an introverted George want a change in personality. There are times when people seem to want a quick and drastic change, but what they truly need is an intentional improvement in the status quo. With the following tips, perhaps you'll start to understand that getting hold of yourself is what truly matters at the end.

Tips to help stay in control of your introversion

Think your thoughts out loud

Sharing is love. Everyone feels loved when given a gift. You can give of your time, energy and words. Mostly, your words are the smallest but strongest gifts you can give to anyone. Let your thoughts out even if it seems odd and feels weird at first. In that way, you can have a good edge over the strong influence of solitude. You know what is always intriguing? Things that seem quite out of the ordinary. If your thoughts and imaginings are perceived by you as bewildering, don't shut them inside, instead talk about them. If you feel empathetic about a situation or toward someone, be sure to head over and offer a listening ear. Don't feel responsible for the incident. Letting out honest words from your heart and hearing yourself say them out loud might just be the reassurance you need to keep you steadfast in all the ways that you are striving to do better. Know that your thoughts will only keep lurking deep inside of you for as long as you shut them in.

- *"I'm the only introvert in a family full of extroverts. I love them but they sap my energy. They're always hosting events, throwing parties or inviting me to one event or the other. They don't take no for an answer and it makes me resent them. Sure, sometimes I enjoy spending time with them but most times, I'm moody and tired when I have to go out for these events."* ~ Sylvia, 22.

Introverts are like fireflies. One second, they sparkle while the next moment the light goes dim and eventually turns off. The fact that your moods seem to be like a car trying to accelerate on a dirt road horribly filled with potholes shouldn't cause you to feel totally out of control. There's no better way to deal with a family of extroverts than educating them on why you need time to recharge. Family is important, try to find a balance between your private time and socializing.

Find, expand and strengthen your social ties

- *"A few years ago, I couldn't keep up with social calls and gatherings. Later on, I realized that I needed to be there for people I truly cared about. To show that I cared, I had to keep up the effort to answer their invitations. I started with the most exciting ones. Weddings! Later, I began attending get togethers, parties and picnics. Then, it just happened. I developed an interest in social outings. It did take some time though."* ~ Williams. 32

As an introvert, flexing your social muscles requires intense determination and a strong will. What if you have no social circle at all? Realistically, that's almost impossible. There is always family and a few friends. Truth is, you can't be there for everyone. Just in case you ever decide to expand your social circle, don't go running after anyone that seems cool. Start off with family, neighbour, workmates and maybe your favourite superstore attendants. Expanding your social circles shouldn't be a game, you need to want to care for those you'll be meeting with.

A broad smile accompanied by the mention of their name with no undertones to your greeting will get your neighbors and colleagues interested in talking with you. Also, do your best not to forget people's names. People will take you seriously when you remember little details about them. Go out more. Don't wait to be invited, take the initiative and take a couple of friends out for a movie or a drink. If at first you feel worried about testing the waters of the extrovert world, you can always bring your social circle home and try to enjoy the comfort that comes from being around people who care about you.

Overcoming the drawbacks of introversion won't come easy, but it will definitely make your life more meaningful if you at least try. Remember, you're not trying to lose your personality, you're only trying to keep it under control and live beyond its so-called restrictions.

Chapter 6

Introvert Issues: Own and Tackle your problems

This chapter will discuss some of the issues that introverts face and how they can tackle it.

Introvert "satellites"

Loneliness

A lot of people suffer from loneliness. They feel lonely not because they chose to. As a matter of fact, most lonely people are never alone. They are often surrounded by their loved ones. But still, loneliness finds a way in, and some people don't even get to know how deeply it has been eating at them until it gets so deeply entrenched that it can no longer be ignored. We say solitude is the hallmark of many introverts. True, solitude every now and then is necessary for introverts to thrive. Nonetheless, they too experience various degrees of loneliness. Some get lonely because they have found too much comfort in their solitude, are spending too much time alone, and fail to realize that humans are programmed to need other humans. We are social beings. For these introverts, what was supposed to be their refuge when the outside world gets too hard has become their prison. These types of introverts turn down all social invitations to the point where people may not invite them anymore. Other introverts may feel lonely not because of a lack of human contact or social interactions, but because they do not feel a connection with what is going on around them. Introverts are generally intuitive and feel deeply; hence, when they deem an event to be too 'shallow' they may choose not to attend.

Does this mean Introverts should abandon their innate nature that craves solitude? Absolutely not!

Introverts need to know that alone time with a great book and a beverage will get you feeling fulfilled on some days, but it won't suffice if you want to live a fulfilled life. There will be days when you have to work at using that 'introvert battery' that you've fully charged by doing things you wouldn't normally do. Go to that party and aim to enjoy yourself, visit loved ones, have people over. Yes, your battery will probably run out and you may end up with an 'introvert hangover', the extreme exhaustion that many introverts feel after participating in extrovert like activities. You may feel exhausted, but being around people can greatly improve your quality of life.

Anxiety

Many introverts suffer from anxiety. Whether it is anxiety about speaking in public, an upcoming work event, or other life issues, it is important that you know that anxiety can be managed successfully. While you should seek professional help for chronic anxiety, there are little things you can do to manage the normal aspects of life that can cause anxiety. Things like meditation and breathing exercises can reduce feelings of anxiety. Also, keeping a journal can be beneficial. In your journal, try to address why you are anxious, ask yourself tough questions and try to answer them. Most of all, be kind to yourself. Realize that nobody has it completely figured out. Take one day at a time.

Over thinking

Over thinking as an introvert is only normal. While it is okay to think things through, it is not okay to over think. Why? Because the more you over think, the less likely you are to go through with whatever it is you are considering. Introverts should try to understand that there will always be things that can go wrong with any endeavour and try to just get started and move forward.

Depression

Sadness is real and it's also an aspect of our lives that we stumble over and deal with frequently. Sometimes, overcoming it makes us stronger, other times, its irrevocable effects are disheartening. In many instances, sadness is alleviated only when it is acknowledged and properly dealt with. But that works perfectly only when one knows the source of their unhappiness. What about the persistent feeling of sadness often resulting from no obvious cause?

Introverted and depressed

There has always been a very nonfactual notion about some sort of mutualism between introversion and depression. From the preceding chapters, we can clearly see how unrealistic the supposed connection between introversion and depression is. Not every depressed person is an introvert. And not every introvert is depressed. Depression occurs randomly among people of various personalities. In spite of that, dealing with depression as an introvert can be exceptionally challenging.

Introverted depressed people hardly ever try to reach out for help. For them, depression might seem a bit subtle at first and is expected to disappear after a while. Surprisingly, people hardly notice the signs of depression in an introvert because of his natural love for solitude. The fact is, many people do not understand what happiness looks like in an introvert. Therefore, when an introvert is depressed, they find it hard to tell the difference. What then is the difference?

When depressed, introverts lose interest in all they cared for. None of the activities that previously held their affection is strong enough to get them out of their misery. The only thing that stays the same is their need for solitude. Often, an excessive need for solitude sets in. Depression renders an introvert nonfunctional in every sense of the word.

Handling depression as an introvert

As they say, change is inevitable. For depression, it only gets worse. Dealing with depression despite your introversive tendencies can be insanely hard. But you can do it! You can fight it off. Depression only becomes stronger when it's neglected and not properly managed. First, get professional help.

If possible, try to uncover the underlying cause of your sadness or factors that exacerbate it.

Savor the moments of triumph

Savoring the littlest moments of triumph over depression can help strengthen and prepare the mind to achieve another feat. Don't be confused, this isn't like singing a victory song while in battle. No. It's like screaming for reinforcements even when winning the battle. So take your time, appreciate the progress you might have made against depression.

Other things you can do to help you include:

- Getting a pet. It is a well-known fact that pets can improve one's mood.

- Exercise. Whether it be cardio or yoga, exercising has proven to bring countless benefits to people suffering from depression.

- Volunteering. There are many studies that show how volunteering can benefit people who are depressed.

How to own and curb your insecurities

There are many ways to go about managing anxiety. Severe cases of anxiety might require medical attention. Generally minor challenges that cause anxiety can be handled with therapy and counsel. However, you can start off with the basics for dealing with anxiety that are given below.

- ACCEPTANCE

Accept and own your feelings of insecurity. Don't push them away, let yourself feel them. You can only be in charge of the things that you own.

- TAKE CHARGE

When you start to feel in charge of your issues, the ability to make decisions that would help you stay in control of them will blossom.

-SAY NO WHEN NECESSARY

There are times when you just have to say NO to things or people that threaten to increase your feelings of insecurity. Learn to say NO from time to time even when you feel guilty for saying it.

-SPREAD THE WORD

There are many people who would treat you better if only they knew about your plight. This isn't a fairy tale, no one has a magic potion that will make your worries disappear. But wholesome words from friends and family might just be the inspiration you need to stand firm. So talk about your fears. It's not taboo to make them known so that others can help you.

- IMPROVE YOUR LIFESTYLE

Making changes in one's life can be troubling at first, but they will be worthwhile in the end. Don't worry if you feel some distress as you begin to make changes in your life. Sometimes all we need to do in order to get off the hook of stress and feel a bit at peace with our life, is make the needed change and try doing things differently. Get organized, read good books, listen to wholesome music, eat healthy meals, and maybe hit the gym. Do better, be better.

www.ingramcontent.com/pod-product-compliance
Lightning Source LLC
Chambersburg PA
CBHW070935220526

45468CB00005B/1780